TDD: How to Do it Properly and Why It's Easy

A short practical guide you can apply right away

Fiodar Sazanavets

TDD: How to Do it Properly and Why It's Easy

A short practical guide you can apply right away

Fiodar Sazanavets

Leanpub

This is a Leanpub book. Leanpub empowers authors and publishers with the Lean Publishing process. Lean Publishing is the act of publishing an in-progress ebook using lightweight tools and many iterations to get reader feedback, pivot until you have the right book and build traction once you do.

Also By Fiodar Sazanavets

The easiest way to become a software developer
The easiest way to learn design patterns
The easiest way to learn design patterns
SignalR on .NET 6 - the Complete Guide

Contents

Getting Started

Test-driven development (TDD) evolved into a complicated topic. If you go online and search for blog posts on what TDD is, you will find as many different opinions as search results. Some of these opinions will make sense. Others will not make any sense at all.

However, TDD is not complicated at all. It only consists of a handful of fundamental principles that can be learned very quickly and applied right away. And this is exactly what this booklet aims to do.

We won't be talking about the philosophy and history of TDD. We won't be arguing about different TDD approaches. We won't be addressing arguments for and against using TDD. I will simply explain to you what works in such a way that you can apply it right away.

This book will show you the following:

- What TDD rules are as defined by proper authoritative sources
- How to do TDD with some practical examples
- What are the TDD practices that work best and why they work best

That's it. That's all you need to know.

If you then want to expand your knowledge of TDD, you can, of course, read some good books and blog posts. By the end of this booklet, I will show you which specific books and online articles you can look at. But you don't have to, as the principles described in this booklet are more than sufficient to get you started.

Prerequisites

Of course, before you can apply TDD, you need to know how to code. So, at the very least, you need to know the following before reading this booklet:

- Being able to use at least one programming language
- Being familiar with at least one unit testing framework

You can, of course, still read this booklet as you are learning how to program or as you are learning how to write automated tests. This may still work. However, you may experience some difficulties understanding the material if you have no prior coding experience.

Practical examples

To ensure that as many people benefit from this booklet as possible, we don't focus on any specific programming language. Therefore, all practical examples are provided in pseudocode.

You should still be able to implement the principles in a concrete programming language of your choice.

The Fundamental Rules of TDD

Before we can do TDD, we need to know exactly what it is. Let's get straight to it and outline the fundamental TDD rules as described by people who are considered to be the authority on the subject and who were involved in developing TDD as a concept.

Different authors described TDD from different angles and to understand TDD properly, you need to be familiar with all of these. Knowing only one set of rules will make your understanding of TDD incomplete and may even make you fill the gaps in your knowledge with incorrect assumptions.

But don't worry, even though there are multiple sets of rules, there are still only a handful of rules in total.

Also, don't worry if you don't immediately understand these rules. Not everyone comprehends them straight away and it's absolutely fine. You can always come back to this section once you have gone through some practical examples. Once you tried TDD yourself, these rules should be easy to comprehend.

Kent Beck's TDD rules

Kent Beck is considered to be one of the most authoritative authors on the subject of TDD. He is the author of the "Test-Driven Development by Example" book, which is considered to be de-facto the TDD Bible.

Here are the five rules[1] that provide a canonical description of TDD according to Kent Beck:

1. Write a list of the test scenarios you want to cover
2. Turn exactly one item on the list into an actual, concrete, runnable test
3. Change the code to make the test (& all previous tests) pass (adding items to the list as you discover them)
4. Optionally refactor to improve the implementation design
5. Until the list is empty, go back to #2

This provides a fairly good description of what the TDD process is supposed to look like. However, this explanation has some gaps. For example, by reading this, it won't be very clear that steps 2 and 3 may have to be repeated multiple times for the same test.

Here is where the three rules of Uncle Bob come in.

---

[1] https://tidyfirst.substack.com/p/canon-tdd

Uncle Bob's TDD rules

Robert Cecil Martin, commonly known as Uncle Bod, is the author of the "Clean Code" book that has been setting the principles of coding best practices for over a decade. He is also considered to be one of the most authoritative figures in the world of TDD. His three rules[2] of TDD are as follows:

1. You are not allowed to write any production code unless it is to make a failing unit test pass.
2. You are not allowed to write any more of a unit test than is sufficient to fail; and compilation failures are failures.
3. You are not allowed to write any more production code than is sufficient to pass the one failing unit test.

Now, it makes a bit more sense. You don't just write a test and then write the implementation. You write your test until you can't write it anymore due to the lack of implementation. Then you add just enough implementation to make the test compile. Then, if needed, you add some additional bits to your test that you couldn't add before. Then, you come back to the implementation and add any missing parts that are required to make the test pass.

---

[2]http://butunclebob.com/ArticleS.UncleBob.TheThreeRulesOfTdd

Industry-standard TDD flow

Based on these rules, the TDD flow can be summarized as consisting of three stages, which were defined by the industry as "Red", "Green", and "Refactor". Here is what they are:

- **Red**: You write a test before any implementation exists. It fails because there is no implementation of the behavior we are trying to test.
- **Green**: You write the implementation to make the test pass.
- **Refactor**: You make your code cleaner and prettier so it's more readable and maintainable without any further changes to the behavior.

Conclusion

Without knowing these three sets of rules, your understanding of TDD will be incomplete. However, if you read them carefully, you might have spotted that there is a contradiction.

The third rule of Uncle Bob, which states that you don't write more code than is sufficient to pass a test goes against the fourth rule of Kent Beck, which is the same as the "Refactor" stage of the industry-standard TDD flow.

This contradiction proves that TDD is supposed to be a guideline to follow and not a set of immutable laws that must be followed at all times. Nevertheless, TDD is still extremely useful, as you shall see next.

A Practical Example of TDD

So, let's see how you may go about doing TDD. Imagine a scenario where you need to build a library that converts markdown (MD) text format into HTML. It's not difficult to imagine use cases for such functionality. This is what GitHub does when it displays README files in the repositories.

For those who are unfamiliar with the markdown format, this guide[1] will help you understand it.

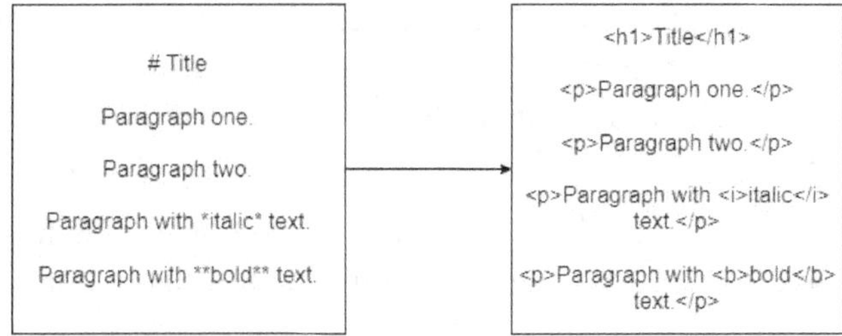

So, let's build this library by applying the TDD approach.

Step 1: Outlining the test cases

We will start by creating a list of all test cases for the behavior we want to implement. This is where many people get confused. Test cases are not the same as executable tests. Those come later. Test cases are brief descriptions of what you expect to happen in each scenario. Here are some examples of test cases:

---

[1]https://www.markdownguide.org/cheat-sheet/

- If an empty string is passed as an input, an empty string is returned
- If the input string starts with the # character followed by a phrase, the output string will not contain the # character, and the phrase will be inside the <h1> HTML tag

The important thing to remember is that we are focusing on only one type of behavior. If our goal is to build a piece of software with multiple functionalities, we will only focus on one functionality at a time. This will help us to avoid context-switching and may even help us to enter the state of flow.

How to come up with test cases

First, we need to think of the base case. In our example, this would be an input string that is either null or empty. Having an input string consisting entirely of whitespaces may also be considered a type of base case.

Then we need to think about what else our software will need to be able to do. So, we will come up with the following test cases:

- Wrappig text paragraphs in the <p> HTML elements.
- Applying appropriate header elements to the lines that start with the # character (<h1> for #, <h2> for ##, and so on).
- Converting blank lines into the <br/> elements.
- Replacing any special character combinations (e.g. *, **, etc.) with the equivalent HTML tags (e.g. <i>, <b>, etc.). We may want to have a separate test case for a separate character combination.

Edge cases

Then we need to think of edge cases. We may, for example, want to limit the size of the input the library can deal with and throw an exception if the input exceeds this size. For this, we will need to create at least two more test cases that will validate the so-called "boundary condition". This is how they will be structured:

- The first test case provides an input that fits within the maximum allowed size and expects a valid output to be returned.
- The second test case exceeds the allowed size by a single character and verifies that an exception of a particular type is thrown.

In this example, we may come up with quite a sizeable list of test cases. Even though it's only a single behavior, we are still dealing with many different types of special characters. We are now ready to turn each of the test cases into concrete executable tests.

> **Note**: If you only follow this step and disregard any other rules of TDD, you will probably still find that your code ends up much cleaner and much fewer bugs creep in.

Step 1: Writing tests

Now, we can start writing the actual executable tests. Remember the first rule of Uncle Bob that forbids us from writing any production code if we don't have tests that cover it? Since we are starting from scratch, to fulfill this rule, we will write the test library first.

So, we create a library that will contain our tests. Then we will have a code file that will contain the executable test methods. Then, we will start writing our first test.

A good way to start is to create a test method (or a function, depending on your programming language) for the test. Then we can specify the expected input and expected output.

There are several naming conventions we can use to name the method. Any will work as long as the name sufficiently describes what behavior we are testing. So here is a pseudocode representation of the logic we would have written:

```
whenEmptyStringIsPassed_ConvertMethodReturnsEmptyString()\
  {

      input = ""
      expectedOutput = ""


  }
```

Before we continue, there is one thing to consider.

Parametrized tests

Most of the testing frameworks support parametrized tests. Those types of tests are preferred as they allow us to test multiple scenarios without having to duplicate code.

If we look at the list of test cases we came up with in the previous section, we will see that all of them but one are very similar to each other:

- They all have a specific input to validate the functionality
- They have the expected output we are comparing the actual output against

The final test case that represents a boundary condition is different. Instead of checking the output, we are checking that the method throws an exception when the length of the input string exceeds the maximum allowed value.

This final test case would still be represented by a non-parametrized test method. But all other test cases can be easily represented by a single parametrized test. So, if our testing framework allows parametrized tests, we will rewrite our test method to look as follows:

```
[TestCase("", "")]
convertMethodReturnsExpectedInput(input, expectedOutput) \
{

}
```

If we do it this way, then for every new test scenario we will just add another test case attribute with another set of values. We won't have to rewrite the code inside the method.

Adding non-compilable code

Next, we will write the invocation of the method we are testing. Let's imagine we intend to have a class called MdToHtmlConverter and it has a static method called convert() that accepts a string parameter and returns a string. So, our test method will now look as follows:

```
1   [TestCase("", "")]
2   convertMethodReturnsExpectedInput(input, expectedOutput) \
3   {
4
5       actualOutput = MdToHtmlConverter.convert(input)
6
7   }
```

Now, we have a problem. Our code will no longer compile. Now, it's time to fulfill the second rule of Uncle Bob, as we are not allowed to write more of the test code than is sufficient to fail. Now, it's time to write the actual implementation to make the code compilable.

> **Note**: With some programming languages and development tools, you may find that writing the code that invokes a method that doesn't yet exist causes you some inconvenience. The auto-complete feature of the code editor may try to replace the code you wrote with something that sounds vaguely similar but represents something completely different. If this happens, It's OK to comment the uncompilable code out and add the implementation before uncommenting it. This will not strictly adhere to the rules of TDD, but the outcome would still be the same.

Step 2: Writing the initial implementation

Now, we will create a library for our production code. Inside this library, we will create a class called MdToHtmlConverter. Inside this class, we will create the convert() method. We will populate this method with the most basic code sufficient for making it compile. So our method will look as follows:

```
1   convert(input) {
2
3       return input
4
5   }
```

Once we've done it, we can come back to our test and complete it.
Before we do it, we need to make sure that our test library references our newly created implementation library and our test call
references the namespace of the newly created MdToHtmlConverter
class.

Completing the test

We left our test in an incomplete state. But in this state, it doesn't
really test anything. To make it useful, we need to add the so-called
assertion.

In automated testing, assertions are used to compare the expected
state with the actual state after executing the piece of functionality
we are testing. The following pseudocode example shows what this
may look like in our test:

```
1   [TestCase("", "")]
2   convertMethodReturnsExpectedInput(input, expectedOutput) \
3   {
4
5       actualOutput = MdToHtmlConverter.convert(input)
6
7       assert.equal(expectedOutput, actualOutput)
8
9   }
```

Assertion will throw an exception if the values don't adhere to the
condition specified, which will make the test fail. In our example,
the condition is that the expected output matches the actual output.

We have now completed our first scenario and reached the Green state where the test passes. We can skip the Refactor phase in this scenario as there is not much to refactor. We can continue with the next test case.

Adding the next test

The goal of our next test case is to validate that the text without any special characters is wrapped in the <p> tag. Parametrized tests allow us to add the test case without writing any new test logic. Our existing test method will now look similar to the following:

```
[TestCase("", "")]
[TestCase("This is a paragraph.", "<p>This is a paragraph\
.</p>")]
convertMethodReturnsExpectedInput(input, expectedOutput) \
{

    actualOutput = MdToHtmlConverter.convert(input)

    assert.equal(expectedOutput, actualOutput)

}
```

Inevitably, this test will fail. Our current production code will merely return the original input. Therefore, the output of `This is a paragraph.` will not match the expected output of `<p>This is a paragraph.</p>`.

We are in the Red stage. We need to modify our implementation to get back to Green.

Fixing the implementation to make the test pass

We can now go back to our convert() method and modify its logic to be similar to the following:

```
1   convert(input) {
2
3       if (input == "")
4           return input
5
6       Split text into paragraphs
7
8       for each paragraph
9           surround the text in <p> and </p>
10
11      Combine the paragraphs
12      Return the combined result
13  }
```

Now, our test will pass. We may or may not want to refactor it. We will then need to keep repeating the process until we run out of test cases and our code is sufficiently readable and maintainable.

What is the Scope of a Test in TDD?

As we saw in our practical example, TDD is where we use tests to write our development. But how do we decide the scope of each test?

Let's find out.

Introduction to testing pyramid

Different types of tests are run at different levels. They can broadly be separated into three distinct categories:

- **End-to-end tests**: They are executed against a deployed application and involve the entire ecosystem. For example, in the scope of such a test, we would interact with the user interface, which will then submit the request to the server, which will then interact with the database and maybe interact with other services too. These tests are slow because they use real network communication and involve many moving parts.
- **Integration tests**: These tests are executed against a single component of an application and involve real networking. For example, if our application is accessible via HTTP, the test will make an HTTP request. However, the application doesn't have to be deployed as a part of the whole ecosystem. Other external connections can be replaced with fakes.
- **Unit tests**: These tests only deal with direct invocation of methods and functions. Because they don't utilize any external resources, they are very fast.

These tests can be represented by the so-called "testing pyramid" displayed in the following figure:

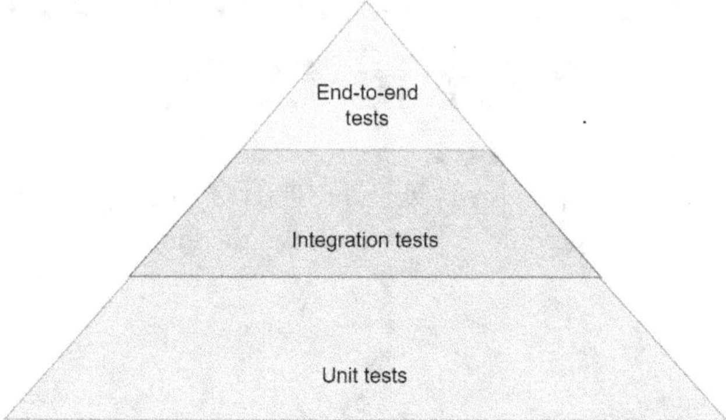

Here is why a pyramid-shaped representation is appropriate:

- We have unit tests at the base because they are fast and we have many of them.
- We have integration tests in the middle because they are somewhat slower and we have fewer of them.
- We have end-to-end tests on the top because they are the slowest and we have relatively few of them.

So, can we use all of these tests to drive development in TDD? The answer is no. Let's see why.

The scope of TDD

If we look at the test pyramid, it becomes apparent that we probably cannot use end-to-end tests in TDD. The scope of such a test is very large but the point of TDD is to get quick and frequent feedback during the development. Of course, these tests are still useful and we should use them. However, we can't use them to "drive" our development.

Unit tests are an obviously good fit for TDD, as these tests deal with smaller units of code. But what about the integration tests? Well, the answer here is "it depends".

Not all integration tests are made equal. If an integration test can run against the code the same way unit tests can be run, then we can use integration tests for TDD. In this configuration, integration tests are almost indistinguishable from unit tests. The only difference is that the integration tests use real or emulated networking. After all, we can use such a test for quick and frequent feedback.

Example of defining the scope of tests

Imagine that we have to develop a REST API that is used for management of the user information. The first endpoint would have the URL path of `/api/users` and it returns the full list of the users currently registered in the system. How do we decide what kind of tests to use to develop such an endpoint?

In this case, if the test framework we use can make a call to the URL paths of the application without having to deploy this application on a dedicated server, we will start with the integration test. So, we can write a test similar to this:

```
1   userEndpointIsOperational() {
2
3       expectedResponseCode = 200;
4
5       response = client.httpGet("/api/users")
6
7       assert.Equal(expectedResponseCode, response.code)
8   }
```

This test will fail until we build an implementation for
this endpoint. We can, for example, create a class called
UsersController. This class relies on another class called
UsersRepository which is represented by the global userRepo
variable. Inside the UsersController class, we may have the
following method mapped to this HTTP endpoint:

```
1   mapGetUsers("/api/users", () {
2
3       return Ok(userRepo.getUsers()))
4
5   })
```

The UsersRepository class will have all the necessary interactions
with the database. Having this interaction inside a separate class
and not inside the controller has many benefits, some of which are
as follows:

- The controller class which has the HTTP endpoint mappings
  acts purely as an adapter layer
- We can run unit tests directly against the getUsers() method
  without involving the HTTP endpoint, so we can have as
  many unit tests against it as would be necessary to cover all
  scenarios.

You may ask at this point: "Why not run unit tests directly against the `mapGetUsers()` method of the `UsersController` class?". Well, there are some good reasons to do things the way we did, some of which are as follows:

- On some frameworks, it may not even be possible, which makes it immediately obvious why we should move the business logic out of the adapter.
- Methods that map to any networked communication protocols, such as HTTP or gRPC, are never invoked directly by our code; therefore the test will be doing something the production code never does.
- We may accidentally apply the incorrect structure to our method which would prevent it from mapping to the endpoint correctly. In this case, our test will pass, but our actual endpoint will not work.

Note: When you use integration tests in TDD, don't use too many of them. You can still validate a wide renge of scenarios by using unit tests. Otherwise, your test pipeline will become slow as it grows large.

What is the "unit"?

In our example, one of our classes depended on another class. This class, in turn, may depend on yet another class for its functionality. There may be many layers of dependencies.

So, what would be the scope of each unit test? Will we apply it to a single method, or would it be OK to traverse the entire dependency tree? Each of these approaches has its pros and cons, but the most effective way is to apply your test to the highest possible level. In this case, an individual test may traverse multiple levels of dependencies.

Here are some benefits of using this approach:

- If you have to refactor the inner logic and reorganize your inner code, you will not have to rewrite your tests.
- Refactoring is about improving your code without making any changes in the behavior. Having a test at a high level will help you to validate that you haven't accidentally changed the behavior.
- You won't have to write too many tests.

In the context of unit tests, the "unit" can be seen as a "unit of behavior" rather than a "unit of implementation". A "unit of implementation" is an individual method or a function. A "unit of behavior", however, may span many individual methods and/or functions.

However, sometimes it still makes sense to go down a level.

The concept of gears

Sometimes, it's not viable to have all of your tests at a high level. For example, your inner code may have to deal with many moving parts and complex conditional logic. Sometimes, it makes more sense to assess different components of this logic individually.

If you find that writing tests at a high level is hard, you can start writing tests at a lower level. This is analogous to shifting gears in a car. Sometimes you have to shift up, while in other situations you would shift down.

Just try not to go too low. Otherwise, you will have too many tests that are brittle and depend too much on the implementation details. Changing implementation details will force you to rewrite those tests.

Mocking: Testing the Untestable

Sometimes, while doing TDD, you will find that some parts of your code are hard to write while being constrained by the rules of TDD. For example, your code may have to submit a HTTP request to an external system.

In this situation, it would be hard to write the code that makes the test pass, especially if the external resource doesn't exist. Even if it did exist, the code would use real networking, so such a test would be slow. Also, because we are relying on an external resource, such a test would be unstable, as this resource is not under our direct control.

However, we shouldn't despair. There is a solution to such a problem. It's called mocking.

Mocking basics

Mocking is when we substitute a real object in our code with a fake object that implements the same interface. Our code will still be able to interact with the mocked object the same way it would be able to interact with a real one.

Mocked objects can also be set up to mimic specific types of behavior exhibited by the real object. For example, an object representing an HTTP client can be set up to pretend to return a response from an HTTP endpoint without interacting with any network.

Mocking example

Let's imagine that one of our classes relies on an interface that represents an HTTP client. We would pass this interface into the constructor of the class.

Here is a pseudocode representation of this class:

```
class UserFacade {

    _client

    UserFacde(IHttpClient client) {

        _client = client

    }

    getUsers() {

        response = _client.get("/api/users")
```

```
14
15            if (response.isSuccessStatusCode)
16                return response.body
17            else
18                return []
19
20        }
21    }
```

We have the getUsers() method in this class that returns a list of users that was retrieved from an external API via an HTTP client. If the response code received from the API doesn't indicate success, the method returns an empty list.

In our normal mode of operation, the IHttpClient interface will be mapped to a concrete implementation that uses real networking and makes a real HTTP request. But in our tests, we can create a dynamic implementation of this interface by using a mocking library available with the programming language and the framework you are using.

Here is how a mock can be set up done inside a test:

```
1   getUsers_returnsUsers() {
2
3       mockClient = mock(IHttpClient)
4
5       response = mock(Response)
6       response.isSuccessStatusCode.returns(true)
7       response.body.returns([
8           new User("Mike Bailey"),
9           new User("Jordan Brown")])
10
11      mockClient.response.returns(response)
12
13      userFacade = new UserFacade(mockClient)
```

```
14
15        users = userFacade.getUsers()
16
17        assert.equal(2, users.length)
18
19    }
```

Here is what we are doing in this test:

1. We are creating a mocked object representing an `IHttpClient` implementation
2. We are creating a mocked representation of a `Response` object
3. We are setting the `isSuccessStatusCode` property of the response object to return `true`
4. We are setting the `body` property of the response object to return a collection of two `User` objects
5. We are setting the `response` property of the mocked HTTP client object to return the mocked response
6. We are instantiating the `UserFacade` class while passing the mocked HTTP client into the constructor
7. We are invoking the `getUsers()` method and asserting that the number of the returned objects is the same as expected

Mocking best practices

Remember the third TDD rule of Uncle Bod that doesn't allow us to write any more production code than is necessary to pass a test? It implies that we should keep the code coverage as close to 100% as possible.

Code coverage is the measure of how much of our production code is executed by our tests. Although it may not always be possible to adhere to this rule of TDD and keep the code coverage at 100%, we should still do our best to try.

Based on this, we should try our best not to mock any of our own code. If we have to mock it, then it's not covered by the tests. This implies that we should keep mocking to the minimum and only use it when necessary.

However, the good news is that most of the things that require mocking wouldn't come from our code. They would come from external libraries. It would include the following things:

- Any network communication clients (HTTP, gRPC, Web-Socket, etc.)
- Objects representing database connections
- Specific types of message listeners
- Any other objects that cannot be easily used in the context of unit tests

Therefore, when deciding what to mock, it's best to mock one of these objects from an external library rather than our own wrapper class that uses this object. This way, the coverage of our own code will be 100% or very close to it.

Where to Go From Here

As we discussed earlier, there is way too much contradictory and confusing information about TDD on the internet. Therefore, I would only recommend a few authoritative sources on TDD if you want to learn it in depth.

The first source is the original Kent Beck's book, Test Driven Development: By Example[1]. This is the most authoritative and the most accurate book on TDD.

You can also subscribe to Kent Becks Substack[2] where he constantly writes about TDD and other software development best practices.

While TDD will allow you to write good-quality code, it is not the only thing that you need for writing good-quality code. Therefore, if you want to improve your overall coding skills, here are a few more books I would recommend:

- Clean Code[3] by Uncle Bob
- Clean Architecture[4] by Uncle Bob

There are many more great books, but it should be sufficient as the starting point.

But remember that you won't learn anything if you just read. The most important thing is to practice. Now, you know how to practice. The best thing you can do is apply the approach learned in the booklet while working on real coding projects.

---

[1] https://www.amazon.com/Test-Driven-Development-Addison-Wesley-Signature/dp/0321146530

[2] https://tidyfirst.substack.com/

[3] https://www.amazon.com/Clean-Code-Handbook-Software-Craftsmanship/dp/0132350882/

[4] https://www.amazon.com/Clean-Architecture-Craftsmans-Software-Structure/dp/B08X8H5G2J

Just apply this approach to your next software development task. You should be able to apply this approach right away. After all, this is what the goal of this booklet was.

Happy coding!

Burn Calories and Lose Weight Now

How to Burn Fat like the Calorie King

By: Desiree Osunak

9781632874689

PUBLISHERS NOTES

Disclaimer – Speedy Publishing, LLC

This publication is intended to provide helpful and informative material. It is not intended to diagnose, treat, cure, or prevent any health problem or condition, nor is intended to replace the advice of a physician. No action should be taken solely on the contents of this book. Always consult your physician or qualified health-care professional on any matters regarding your health and before adopting any suggestions in this book or drawing inferences from it.

The author and publisher specifically disclaim all responsibility for any liability, loss or risk, personal or otherwise, which is incurred as a consequence, directly or indirectly, from the use or application of any contents of this book.

Any and all product names referenced within this book are the trademarks of their respective owners. None of these owners have sponsored, authorized, endorsed, or approved this book.

Always read all information provided by the manufacturers' product labels before using their products. The author and publisher are not responsible for claims made by manufacturers.

This book was originally printed before 2014. This is an adapted reprint by Speedy Publishing, LLC with newly updated content designed to help readers with much more accurate and timely information and data.

Speedy Publishing, LLC

40 E Main Street,

Newark

Delaware

19711

Contact Us: 1-888-248-4521

Website: http://www.speedypublishing.com

REPRINTED Paperback Edition: ISBN: 9781632874689

Manufactured in the United States of America